The Sports Devotional

The Sports Devotional

Bryce T. Johnson

30
Days of
Encouragement
for Following
Jesus

invite
PRESS

Plano, Texas

To my mom and dad, who continue to show me what it looks like to follow Jesus. I thank my dad for igniting my passion for sports. I thank them both for supporting me and encouraging me every step along my journey.

Acknowledgments

I praise God for His goodness and faithfulness. I'm grateful that He allows me to know Him personally, and I thank Him for how He leads me and guides me. I thank Jesus for being my Lord and Savior and for the Holy Spirit, who continually works in me and through me.

I'm thankful I get to go home each day to my amazing wife, Jodi, and two sweet daughters, Maddie and Mikayla. They bring so much joy to my life.

The devotionals in this book are inspired by God as He allowed me to see parallels in sports that relate and connect to His Word.

I want to thank the board, staff, and supporters of UNPACKIN' It Ministries. It's a privilege to serve alongside so many wonderful people as we pursue our mission to challenge, encourage, and inspire sports fans to follow Jesus to become more like Him.

This book was a team effort with Matt Osborne and Darla Johnson from UNPACKIN' It Ministries. Their gifts and skills are an ongoing blessing to sports fans. They played a big role in making this book possible.

Thanks to Chris Bryant and Mike Burch for encouraging me to write this book and for their many years of faithful support.

Thanks to Talbot Davis for connecting me to Len Wilson. Thanks to Len Wilson and his team at Invite Resources for their willingness to publish this book and partner in such a significant way. I'm grateful for each person who contributed to the process of bringing this book to life. The entire team worked so hard, and I'm proud to share the finished product with sports fans.

**To find out more about the author
and his ministry, scan here.**

Preface

I'm a huge sports fan and am passionate about Jesus. I enjoy watching sports, going to games, and listening to sports talk. As I do, God reveals to me how sports relate to life and to the Bible. In this book you will find 30 sports stories that point to biblical truth. Jesus used parables and stories to communicate truth. Likewise in this book you will find sports stories that I hope will help make biblical truths become clearer to you as a sports fan.

The book includes 30 days of daily devotionals about sports and life. I hope you will read each devotional, answer the questions for yourself, and pray the prayer that follows. I trust you will be challenged, encouraged, and inspired as a sports fan to follow Jesus and become more like Him. Reflect on what you read each day, read it with another sports fan so you can discuss it together, and look up the context around specific scriptures for further Bible reading.

This book is for every sports fan who desires to take the next step in his or her journey with Jesus, no matter what that starting point is.

NFL Draftees Who Wait

As exciting as it must be for a player to hear his name called during the NFL Draft, waiting for a team to select him must be equally agonizing.

Talented players dream about making it to the league, and scouting experts tell them they are good enough to be picked. However, many players end up waiting much longer than they expected. Some players anticipate going in an earlier round yet don't hear their names called as soon as they had imagined. Then there are the highly touted college players who slip into the latter part of the first round. Although it's hard to feel sorry for them when they're first-rounders, knowing that all eyes are on them as they wait can't be easy for them.

Over the years, some of the big names who had expected to go early but ended up waiting to hear their names called later in the first round include Aaron Rodgers (24th overall), Randy Moss (21st pick), Brady Quinn (22nd selection), and Dan Marino (27th overall).

Even though waiting usually means a player ends up with a better team, he still has to fight against impatience, worry, and disappointment. Players quickly realize that they can't force a team to select them and must humbly accept that they aren't in control.

Just like an NFL draftee, we understand that waiting for something can be brutal. Most of us are either waiting for something right now or have just finished a season of waiting.

No one likes to wait, but when we properly do so, our trust and faith in God significantly grow. We learn patience and humility amid uncertainty and surrender to the fact that so much lies out of our control.

It's usually not until after we get through the delay that we're able to look back on our times of waiting with gratefulness for the work God accomplished in our hearts.

Although God has the power to answer our prayers immediately, He uses these delays to strengthen our dependence on Him. As our dependence grows, so does our love for Him. We turn to God for comfort, hope, and peace.

Romans 12:12 tells us to "rejoice in our confident hope. Be patient in trouble, and keep on praying." We discover freedom in letting go and trusting that God's decisions and plans for our lives are better than our own. We can find peace in knowing that He's in control and His purposes are more important than our desire for quick responses. The worst thing we can do is try to speed up God's work and perfect timing. Instead, we need to wait patiently for Him to reveal His answers and rejoice while we're anticipating them.

Psalm 27:13–14 says, "Yet I am confident I will see the LORD's goodness while I am here in the land of the living. Wait patiently for the LORD. Be brave and courageous. Yes, wait patiently for the LORD."

As hard as it may be, let's wait patiently for the Lord and remember to look back with thanksgiving for how much we've grown. Let's be thankful God's kindness allows us to wait so He can use that time of waiting for our good.

I'm Bryce Johnson, and you can *UNPACK* that!

PRAYER: *Heavenly Father, please give me the strength to wait patiently. On the hard days, help me to lean on You instead of showing impatience. Thank You for using seasons of waiting to develop my character and deepen my reliance on You. I am grateful for Your goodness and faithfulness. In Jesus' name, I pray. Amen.*

In what ways have you grown during a season of waiting?

Why is waiting patiently so important?

DID YOU KNOW

Did you know that the lowest-drafted player to eventually be inducted into the NFL Hall of Fame is Roosevelt Brown, who was selected in the 27th round of the 1953 Draft?

A Busted Bracket

O ne of the highlights of the year for a sports fan is sitting down and filling out an NCAA tournament bracket for March Madness. Going through all the different options, we carefully select our "upset specials," Cinderella stories, and the team we think will cut down the nets at the Final Four. As college basketball fans, we hold out hope that our bracket will be the perfect one, where every game goes exactly how we predicted it.

It typically doesn't take very long for our brackets to be officially busted.

Even though we may feel we have good reasons to think the tournament will go a certain way, we're quickly reminded of how unpredictable the tournament is.

How should we respond to our busted brackets? Should we rip them up, cry, and stop watching the tournament? Or should we admit we have no control over the outcomes and just enjoy the games as they unfold?

My brother got me thinking about this one year when he texted me: "Yeah, once you give up on your bracket, it enables you to cheer for more of the upsets." Let's face it: the upsets are the best part of March Madness!

At some point in our lives, many of us put together a "bracket" for how we want our lives to turn out. We predict we'll get married, work a dream job, live in a nice home, have three kids, and retire on the beach.

Chances are, somewhere along the way our "life brackets" get busted, and what we hope will happen turns out to be several "upsets" instead.

So, here's the question: How do we handle the broken brackets and upsets in life?

I have to go back to the text from my brother: "Yeah, once you give up on your bracket, it enables you to cheer for more of the upsets." The sooner we're willing to surrender our plans for a perfect life, the sooner we're able to freely enjoy the life God has for us. When we "give up on our bracket" by admitting we're not in control, we can stop worrying about wanting everything to go our way and trust God as life unfolds according to His will.

"Trust in the LORD with all your heart," Proverbs 3 encourages us, "and do not lean on your own understanding. In all your ways acknowledge him, and he will make straight your paths" (vv. 5–6 ESV).

We can gain freedom and peace when we rip up our own "bracket" and embrace God's surprises. Admittedly, God uses "upsets" in life to grow our faith, build our character, and reveal His goodness. In the end, they make our journey special. As Paul wrote in 2 Corinthians 12:10 (AMP), "So I am well pleased with weaknesses, with insults, with distresses, with persecutions, and with difficulties, for the sake of Christ; for when I am weak [in human strength], then I am strong [truly able, truly powerful, truly drawing from God's strength]."

Let's be thankful for our "busted brackets," so we can enjoy life even more as we let go of clinging to what we think will be the perfect bracket.

I'm Bryce Johnson, and you can *UNPACK* that!

PRAYER: *Heavenly Father, I know Your way is best and You are in control. I pray my heart will be fully surrendered to You so I can live with more freedom and peace. Thank You for the upsets and challenges in life. I know you're using them for my good. I pray this in Jesus' name. Amen.*

In what ways has your bracket been busted in life?

How have the upsets in life changed you for the better?

DID YOU KNOW

Did you know that only two 16-seeds have ever defeated a 1-seed in the Men's NCAA Tournament: UMBC in 2018 and Fairleigh Dickinson in 2023?

Valuing the Home Run

In 1998, Major League Baseball stars Mark McGwire and Sammy Sosa blasted home runs night after night while breaking Roger Maris' thirty-seven-year-old single-season record for home runs. By the end of that season, Sosa had hit 66 out of the park, and McGwire sent 70 balls over the fence.

As a young sports fan, I enjoyed watching both these players repeatedly hit home runs and made my way to the TV whenever they were at the plate. It was a thrill to see them go for the record at the same time and push each other to do so throughout the summer.

Whether we fans are watching on TV or sitting in the ballpark, nothing gets us out of our seats quite like a ball being crushed by a batter. We are simply captivated by the home run!

Home runs have always been a big deal, but after that incredible summer, young baseball players realized the true value of a home run. In turn, they specifically emphasized being able to hit the long ball and set out to become home run hitters.

Alex Rodriguez once shared, "If you can articulate what you value, and what you're looking for, players of this caliber of athleticism can turn themselves into it. It's kind of standing the test of time, where guys know that runs are valuable, and the ones that have the capability to do it—meaning the strength—are lifting the ball a little bit more and putting more balls in the seats."[1]

I believe this truth about baseball players valuing the home run and becoming home run hitters applies to how we place value in our own lives. As we determine what's most important to us, we also find a correlation to what we're becoming. If we value being a faithful spouse, a loving parent, and a reliable worker, then we'll do what it takes to become or "turn into" those things.

However, that can only truly happen when we first value God and rely on His power to help us become who He created us to be. It's Christ living in us that transforms us from the inside out, enabling us to live godly lives as we become more and more like Him.

If we place our ultimate value and importance on loving, seeking, and serving God and depending on His strength to change our character, then we can become faithful spouses, loving parents, dependable friends, and reliable workers.

First Timothy 4:8 tells us, "While bodily training is of some value, godliness is of value in every way, as it holds promise for the present life and also for the life to come" (ESV).

We can clearly see that Major League Baseball values the home run. When we view our own lives, what do we value? Do we value God and His ways enough to place everything else as secondary?

In Matthew 13:44, Jesus uses the parable of the hidden treasure to shed light on valuing the kingdom of heaven: "The kingdom of heaven is like treasure hidden in a field, which a man found and covered up. Then in his joy, he goes and sells all that he has and buys that field" (ESV).

---

1. Tyler Kepner, "This Season's First Half Was a Home Run Derby," *New York Times*, July 10, 2017, https://www.nytimes.com/2017/07/10/sports/baseball/home-runs-major-leagues-first-half.html.

Are we willing to place our highest value on God and His kingdom and let go of anything else that is less important and getting in the way?

I'm Bryce Johnson, and you can *UNPACK* that!

PRAYER: *Heavenly Father, I know I place value on some things that don't matter. Please help me place the most value on bringing You glory and following Jesus so I can become more like Him. I pray this in Jesus' name. Amen.*

What do you value the most?

How has what you value determined your character and what you've become?

 **DID YOU KNOW**

Did you know Mark McGwire's longest home run during the 1998 season was recorded at 545 feet?

Knowing How to Win

When we reflect on the career of basketball legend Bill Russell, we have no doubt he knew how to win. Russell won eleven NBA titles, two NCAA Championships, two state championships in high school, and an Olympic gold medal during his career.

According to a tweet from ESPN's Paul Hembekides:

> Bill Russell played 21 winner-take-all games in his career (NBA, Olympics, NCAA Tournament).
>
> His teams went 21–0.
>
> 10 of those were NBA Game 7s, and in them, he played 488 of 495 minutes and averaged 29.3 rebounds.[1]

All that Russell accomplished throughout his basketball career is remarkable, and it's unlikely we'll ever see another athlete achieve that type of winning in his or her sport.

Russell knew what it took to win on the basketball court. He put himself in a position to help his team win, and he understood that winning was achieved by being a good teammate and making the players around him better. Despite all his accolades, he never wanted the focus to be on his individual accomplishments.

As we think about Russell knowing how to win on the basketball court, I want to unpack what it means for us to win in life.

---

1. Paul Hembekidesb (Hembo) (@PaulHembo), "Bill Russell played 21 winner-take-all games in his career . . . ," Twitter, July 31, 2022, 12:57 p.m., https://twitter.com/PaulHembo/status/1553802019235930112.

Society has conditioned us to think that it's all about individual accolades, substantial bank accounts, big brands, and large platforms. But just as winning on the basketball court isn't ultimately about an individual's stats, winning in life isn't all about individual success.

Instead, it's about serving others, being a good teammate, and making others better. We put ourselves in a position to experience true wins, blessings, and joy when the focus isn't on ourselves. Winning begins by humbly shifting our attention to God, rooting ourselves in His Word, abiding in Jesus, and following His path.

Psalm 1:1–3 says, "Blessed is the man who walks not in the counsel of the wicked, nor stands in the way of sinners, nor sits in the seat of scoffers; but his delight is in the law of the Lord, and on his law, he meditates day and night. He is like a tree planted by streams of water that yields its fruit in its season, and its leaf does not wither. In all that he does, he prospers" (ESV).

But what does it mean to prosper? The ESV Study Bible note for verse 3 explains, "The first image is that of a **tree** in a dry climate, which nevertheless thrives because of its constant supply of **water.** A tree bears fruit, not for itself, but for others; thus, when the faithful **prospers**, it is not for himself, nor is the prospering even necessarily material, but he succeeds in bringing benefit to others."[2]

When our lives are rooted in God, we will bear fruit and bless others. Proverbs 11:25 gives us this encouragement: "The generous will prosper; those who refresh others will themselves be refreshed."

It seems counterintuitive, but we win when we help others win. Let's be encouraged to follow the example of Jesus, who "did not come to be served, but to serve, and to give his life as a ransom for many" (Matthew 20:28 NIV).

---

2. ESV Study Bible, Personal Size, ESV Bible (Wheaton, IL, Crossway, 2011), 942, note to Ps. 1:3.

He's the ultimate winner thanks to His victory on the cross! I'm Bryce Johnson, and you can *UNPACK* that!

PRAYER: *Heavenly Father, I confess I chase after my own success and personal accolades. I pray You'll change my perspective on what it truly means to win and live a life that is blessed. Help me understand that blessings come from serving and being generous. Teach me to remain rooted in You and delight in Your Word. In Jesus' name, I pray. Amen.*

What has been your perspective on what it takes to win in life?

Who has been a great "teammate" you've been around over the years?

DID YOU KNOW

Did you know Bill Russell holds the record for most rebounds in an NBA Finals game with 40?

Enjoying the Benefits of Voluntary Workouts

Football is a tough sport and a big commitment for players. They must keep their bodies in shape, endure continuous pounding from hits, study playbooks, and diligently practice during the offseason. This requires self-discipline, effort, and intentionality, especially when a workout isn't mandatory.

As part of an agreement between the players and the owners, players are not required to participate in certain activities during the offseason because they're considered "voluntary workouts." Though the players have the freedom to stay home, many players end up joining their teammates for in-person "voluntary workouts," so they can establish team chemistry, improve their skills, spend time with coaches, and demonstrate their commitment to the team.

While each player has been given the freedom to choose not to attend "voluntary workouts," only those who show up take full advantage of the growth opportunities available to them.

When it comes to our own lives as followers of Jesus, we live in freedom because of God's grace and the free gift of salvation. We are securely on His team because of our faith in Jesus and His finished work on the cross, and our spot isn't based on our attendance at "voluntary workouts."

However, as we live on earth as members of God's team, He invites us to participate in "voluntary workouts." They're made available to help us know Him better, become more like Him, develop our faith, establish team chemistry, and demonstrate our commitment to Him.

We can consider "voluntary workouts" as fellowship with other believers, corporate worship, serving at church, praying, meditating on Scripture, studying God's Word, and fasting. God invites us to get to know Him deeply as we seek Him through these different means.

These voluntary workouts are tremendous growth opportunities. They're dedicated time with our Coach and teammates, filled with benefits for those who show up—even though they're not required.

First Timothy 4:8 tells us, "Physical training is good, but training for godliness is much better, promising benefits in this life and in the life to come."

The reality is that if an NFL player loves football, he practices so he can enhance his game. He knows he doesn't necessarily have to, but he wants to because that's how he'll improve his skills.

Likewise, if we love God and desire to follow Jesus, then we want to do what's going to enhance our faith and help us become more like Him. Ultimately, it's God who empowers us and does the transforming work in us.

Paul shares this encouragement in Philippians 2:12–13:

> Continue to work out your salvation [that is, cultivate it, bring it to full effect, actively pursue spiritual maturity] with awe-inspired fear and trembling [using serious caution and critical self-evaluation to avoid anything that might offend God or discredit the name of Christ]. For it is [not your strength, but it is] God who is effectively at work in

you, both to will and to work [that is, strengthening, energizing, and creating in you the longing and the ability to fulfill your purpose] for His good pleasure. (AMP)

Let's voluntarily work out our salvation by relying on the Lord, pursuing Him, serving Him, representing Him, and practicing the spiritual disciplines in which He invites us to freely participate.

I'm Bryce Johnson, and you can *UNPACK* that!

PRAYER: *Heavenly Father, thank You for saving me and giving me new life. I pray I will freely and willingly continue to seek You and participate in everything You have available for me to grow and know You better. In Jesus' name, I pray. Amen.*

What is your perspective on spiritual disciplines like reading and fasting or other "voluntary workouts"?

What holds you back from participating in these growth opportunities?

DID YOU KNOW

Did you know Jerry Rice participated in his own intense voluntary workouts six days a week during the offseason, taking only two weeks off?

Even If Not, I'll Be Okay

T he University of Virginia's men's basketball program has one of the best stories in the history of college basketball.

In 2018, the Cavaliers became the first No. 1 seed in the history of the NCAA Tournament to lose to a 16-seed, falling 74–54 to the University of Maryland, Baltimore County (UMBC. It was a painful and embarrassing result for a team that had been considered a front-runner to win the national championship that season.

Fast-forward one year, however, and the Cavaliers redeemed their historic 2018 loss by winning six consecutive tournament games and becoming the 2019 national champions.

As amazing as that redemption story is, I want to focus on what Virginia head coach Tony Bennett said in a press conference before winning that national championship:

> Going through what we did, losing and all those things, [I told the team that] it created a fire in me that wanted to become a better coach and pursue trying to get these guys to as far as they can, a Final Four, a national championship.
>
> It's burning hot, but it did something I think maybe as significant or greater. It made me realize that if that never does happen, I'll still be OK. Because I've been blessed beyond what I deserve. And I think it's freed me up to go after this as hard as I can, as hard as we can.[1]

---

1. David Jones, "Tony Bennett and Matt Painter Reach for a Final Four, as Mentors

Bennett's comments show us that when we get to a place where being okay isn't based on things going our way, we can finally live with peace, contentment, and satisfaction.

Since we all have our own "Final Four" aspirations, we can easily get frustrated, upset, discouraged, or angry if we are forced to wait for them to come to fruition. But can we get to the point of saying, "If that never does happen, I'll still be okay"?

As followers of Jesus, when our peace and contentment are found in Him, we can be okay regardless of our circumstances.

Paul gives this blessing in 2 Thessalonians 3:16 (AMP): "Now may the Lord of peace Himself grant you His peace at all times and in every way [that peace and spiritual well-being that comes to those who walk with Him, regardless of life's circumstances]. The Lord be with you all."

To take it a step further, there's a powerful story in Daniel 3 where Shadrach, Meshach, and Abednego give this inspirational response before being thrown into a fire for not bowing down to idols: "If it be so, our God whom we serve is able to rescue us from the furnace of blazing fire, and He will rescue us from your hand, O king. But even if He does not, let it be known to you, O king, that we are not going to serve your gods or worship the golden image that you have set up!" (vv. 17–18 AMP).

God can answer our prayers. However, if things turn out differently than we hope, we must remain faithful and filled with peace because, in Jesus, we are always going to be okay.

And as seen in the stories with Coach Bennett and Shadrach, Meshach, and Abednego, often when we get to that genuine point of surrender and contentment, God ends up delivering amazingly.

I'm Bryce Johnson, and you can *UNPACK* that!

Dick Bennett and Gene Keady did 19 Years Ago," Penn Live, Sports, March 30, 2019, https://www.pennlive.com/sports/2019/03/tony-bennett-and-matt-painter-reach-for-a-final-four-as-mentors-dick-bennett-and-gene-keady-did-19-years-ago.html.

PRAYER: *Heavenly Father, I pray I'll get to the point where I'm okay and at peace—even if I don't receive what I want or accomplish all my dreams. Help me to rest in Jesus and praise You regardless of my circumstances. It's in Jesus' name, I pray. Amen.*

Do you have an example of a time when you truly got to the point of saying, "Even if not, I'll be okay"?

What is something you need to surrender to and then declare those words?

DID YOU KNOW

Did you know that Tony Bennett is the all-time winningest coach in the history of Virginia basketball?

Nick Saban Asks Why

The press conferences of Alabama football coach Nick Saban can be highly entertaining. After all, when you have the job security that he does, you can say whatever is on your mind.

Saban regularly goes on funny and passionate rants because he's frustrated with the media. One of his most iconic diatribes involved his thoughts on how the media predicts who is going to win and how well each player is going to do in a given season.

As sports fans, we know this is part of the deal, and we typically join the media in our own prognosticating. But Saban isn't amused by any of this, as he made clear in his response to the media: "Why do we even play? Why do we even have practice? Why do we compete? Why do we coach guys? How they need to improve. I mean, you guys got all the answers to how guys are gonna be, what they're gonna do . . . how good they are . . . So why would you ask me?"[1]

I'm not exactly sure what he hoped to get out of his scolding session at the press conference, and we can certainly laugh off Saban's sarcasm, but I think those questions are reasonable for every player and coach to consider. Asking why someone plays, practices, and competes is something worth pondering.

---

1. ABC News, "Nick Saban: 'Why Do We Even Play? Why Do We Have Practice?'," ABC News, August 17, 2017, https://abcnews.go.com/Sports/nick-saban-play-practice/story?id=49271093.

How about in our own lives? Do we ever consider the why behind our decisions? Do we remember why we married our spouses, why we chose our professions, why we go to work, or why we choose to love and forgive people?

Even more important, do we think about why we follow Jesus, why God sent Him to earth to die, and why it's worth surrendering everything to follow Him?

We don't want to just go through the religious motions without having a reason for doing so. Instead, we need to be motivated by the why behind our devotion to Jesus.

In some ways, these questions lead to unique personal answers, but there are biblical responses to some of these questions, as well.

First John 4:9 explains why Jesus came: "God showed how much he loved us by sending his one and only Son into the world so that we might have eternal life through him."

Verse 11 of the same chapter tells us why we love each other: "Dear friends, since God loved us that much, we surely ought to love each other."

Verses 15 and 16 give us truth about why we obey and love God: "All who declare that Jesus is the Son of God have God living in them, and they live in God. We know how much God loves us, and we have put our trust in his love."

Romans 3:23 affirms why we need a Savior: "For everyone has sinned; we all fall short of God's glorious standard."

Finally, Romans 6:23 tells us why Jesus died and why we're saved: "For the wages of sin is death, but the free gift of God is eternal life in Christ Jesus our Lord."

Let's each contemplate the "whys" in our lives and accept that Jesus is the ultimate answer as He says in John 14:6: "I am the way, the truth, and the life. No one can come to the Father except through me."

I'm Bryce Johnson, and you can *UNPACK* that!

PRAYER: *Heavenly Father, I admit I'm a sinner in need of a Savior and thank You for sending Jesus. I believe Your Word is true and Jesus is who He says He is, so I choose to surrender to Him. It's in His name I pray. Amen.*

What "why" question do you struggle with knowing the answer?

What motivations in your life need to change?

DID YOU KNOW

Did you know that Nick Saban holds the record for most wins against teams ranked in the AP Poll with 104?

Unlearning with the Manning Brothers

One of my favorite parts of recent NFL seasons is watching Peyton and Eli Manning during Monday Night Football. I thoroughly enjoy their humor, insight, and tremendous brotherly banter. I don't want to miss a moment of the entertaining and captivating conversations between Peyton and Eli and their guests.

In one of their first games together, the brothers were talking about a quarterback who had been traded to a new team. Eli asked his older brother, "What do you think the hardest part is about going to a new system? You've been in one system for a long time, and all of a sudden you get a new one."

Peyton responded, "It's unlearning your old system." He then explained how plays are called a certain way with the old team, but then a different terminology has to be learned with the new team. He further explained that because the names of those plays and audibles have been called for so many years, a quarterback sometimes calls out an old one and his new teammates don't know what he's saying.

Super Bowl champion Matthew Stafford shared that sentiment when he talked with the Mannings about his experience going to a new team: "It is a big adjustment. You know, people think it's just learning a new system. I think the biggest thing and the toughest thing for me is forgetting the old one."[1]

The concept of unlearning is also critical in our own lives. There are ways we think, act, and speak when we're single that change when we're married, and then change again when we're parents.

But even more significant is unlearning from a spiritual standpoint. When we receive Jesus Christ as our Lord and Savior and the Holy Spirit comes into our lives, we begin the process of transformation. We embark on a new life with God and "step into a new system" as we continue to learn His ways.

It can be challenging as we live our new lives because of having spent so much time in an "old system." These behaviors must be unlearned while we grow in our understanding of the "new system" and embrace the new team we're on.

Our minds and hearts must change, and thankfully, God allows us to learn and unlearn through the power of the Holy Spirit as we leave our former "playbook" behind.

Ephesians 4:21–24 offers us this great encouragement: "Since you have heard about Jesus and have learned the truth that comes from him, throw off your old sinful nature and your former way of life, which is corrupted by lust and deception. Instead, let the Spirit renew your thoughts and attitudes. Put on your new nature, created to be like God—truly righteous and holy."

Romans 12:2 also tells us, "Don't copy the behavior and customs of this world, but let God transform you into a new person by changing the way you think. Then you will learn to know God's will for you, which is good and pleasing and perfect."

---

1.   "Best of Matthew Stafford's Visit with the Manning Brothers on Monday Night Football / Week 3, TheRams.com, September 28, 2021, https://www.therams.com/video/best-matthew-stafford-eli-peyton-manning-monday-night-football.

Let's praise God that we've been given a new "system" and as we learn His new ways, let's ask Him to help us unlearn the wrong ways we think, act, believe, and speak.

I'm Bryce Johnson, and you can *UNPACK* that!

PRAYER: *Heavenly Father, thank You for the way You continue to transform me. Please help me unlearn anything that's holding me back from living according to Your will. Please give me new desires, thoughts, and patterns that honor and glorify You. In Jesus' name I pray. Amen.*

What are some of the things you had to unlearn when you began following Jesus?

What are some more recent ways God has helped you think, act, or speak differently as you've matured spiritually?

DID YOU KNOW

Did you know that Peyton Manning never lost to his younger brother in the NFL, going a perfect 3-0 against Eli?

The Curtain of Distraction

ollege basketball fans are creative in the ways they irritate the visiting team. One of my favorite student sections is at Arizona State, where they utilize the "Curtain of Distraction" on the front row behind the basket.

Two fans hold up a curtain throughout the game, waiting for the opposing team to visit the free-throw line. When the player steps up and receives the ball, the curtain is dramatically removed with the hope of causing the free-throw shooter to miss.

What happens once the curtain is dropped is hilarious and clever. Sometimes students will wear masks, dress up as Disney characters, or even rub mayonnaise on their chests.

The shooter can't help but notice the shenanigans taking place—especially when an actor, Indy car racer, MLB pitcher, or Olympic swimmer appears behind the curtain. Former NBA star Grant Hill once surprised students by making an appearance.

It's hard to quantify exactly how much all of this affects an opponent's ability to make free throws, but some studies have revealed a one- to three-point advantage for Arizona State.

For a free-throw shooter not to get rattled by the Curtain of Distraction, he must concentrate and continue thinking about making the shot. As soon as his attention shifts to whatever is behind the curtain, that free throw becomes a lot tougher to make.

Each day we are surrounded by our own "Curtain of Distraction," which is designed to cause our eyes and minds to wander. At home, instead of engaging with our families, we're busy thinking about work. At work, we're distracted because we focus on what's wrong with our jobs instead of concentrating on God using us for His purposes while we work.

If we aren't careful, the distraction of attractive people can take our eyes off our spouses. Not to mention the countless other ways we're distracted by technology, social media, and busyness.

Ultimately, it's a battle of our minds as we fight distractions and avoid getting sucked in.

This is especially critical in our spiritual lives, as we can easily get distracted by the world and all that it offers. We lose sight of what's most important and ultimately what God desires for us.

To fight well against the Curtain of Distraction, we need to use God's Word as the lens through which we view distractions.

Philippians 4:8 says, "Finally, brothers, whatever is true, whatever is honorable, whatever is just, whatever is pure, whatever is lovely, whatever is commendable, if there is any excellence, if there is anything worthy of praise, think about these things" (ESV).

Keeping our eyes on Jesus instead of on the distractions from the world is also crucial. Hebrews 12:1–2 encourages us, "Let us strip off every weight that slows us down, especially the sin that so easily trips us up. And let us run with endurance the race God has set before us. We do this by keeping our eyes on Jesus, the champion who initiates and perfects our faith."

The "Curtain of Distraction" will be present today, but instead of being rattled by it, let's keep our eyes focused on Jesus. Let's be challenged to replace our distractions with thoughts that draw us closer to Jesus and keep us on His path.

I'm Bryce Johnson, and you can *UNPACK* that!

PRAYER: *Heavenly Father, forgive me for being distracted and thinking about things that don't please You. Please give me the strength needed to keep my eyes on You and my thoughts pure, true, and honorable. In Jesus' name. Amen.*

What distracts you the most during your day?

How do you avoid distractions or not allow them to cause you to lose focus on what's most important?

DID YOU KNOW

Did you know that Missouri State's Blake Ahearn holds the all-time NCAA record for the highest career free throw percentage, making 94.6% of his career attempts?

What Was Your Message to the Team?

When we watch sports on TV, we not only see the action on the field but also listen to sideline reporters throughout the game. These reporters are tasked with interviewing coaches in hopes of getting some revealing comments that provide value to the audience.

One of the most common questions reporters ask before the game is, "What was your message to the team?"

Usually, coaches reveal something they tell the whole team regarding the general game plan and what they want the focus for the entire team to be.

Reporters also ask coaches to share what they told specific players on the sideline. They'll ask a question like, "Coach, when you pulled the quarterback to the side after the interception, what was your message to him?"

Typically, coaches explain how they encourage and challenge players and tell them what needs to change or what they should specifically do.

These dialogues demonstrate that head coaches are speaking with a message for everyone, while also having personalized conversations with individual players.

Head coaches delivering such messages as these relate to how God speaks to us. By providing His Word in the Bible, God gives us

His general game plan for the "team" and what He wants the focus for all of us to be.

God's message of love, hope, grace, obedience, repentance, and salvation through faith in the death and resurrection of Jesus is for all people.

Titus 2:11–14 (ESV) explains, "For the grace of God has appeared, bringing salvation for all people, training us to renounce ungodliness and worldly passions, and to live self-controlled, upright, and godly lives in the present age, waiting for our blessed hope, the appearing of the glory of our great God and Savior Jesus Christ, who gave himself for us to redeem us from all lawlessness and to purify for himself a people for his own possession who are zealous for good works."

As we follow Jesus, God pulls us aside to personally encourage and challenge us, telling us what we individually need to change or what He wants us to specifically do.

When we have personal conversations with God, He conveys to each of us a particular message He wants us to know. He gives us certain tasks and instructions while telling us His unique purpose for us.

Notice how personal Psalm 23:1–3 is: "The LORD is my Shepherd [to feed, to guide and to shield me], I shall not want. He lets me lie down in green pastures; He leads me beside the still and quiet waters. He refreshes and restores my soul (life); He leads me in the paths of righteousness for His name's sake" (AMP).

Just as a head coach doesn't tell an individual player something that goes against the overall team game plan, God isn't going to tell us something contradictory to His Word. When we seek Him, He'll continually remind us of our role in His overall design.

Let's continue to look for God's message to all of us and embrace the personal messages He has for each of us.

I'm Bryce Johnson, and you can *UNPACK* that!

PRAYER: *Heavenly Father, thank You for revealing Yourself to the world and allowing us to know You personally. Help me to understand Your Word better and hear Your messages more clearly. Thank you for the individual purposes and personal instructions You have for me. In Jesus' name I pray. Amen.*

In what ways has God clearly communicated personal instructions for you?

How would you describe your personal fellowship with God?

DID YOU KNOW

Did you know that former Packers coach Vince Lombardi focused on football fundamentals by telling his team at the start of training camp in 1961, "Gentlemen, this is a football."

What If Failure Is the Point?

Tim Tebow had one of the most interesting sports careers of any athlete in history.

After an accomplished college football career, Tebow bounced around to four different NFL teams (Broncos, Patriots, Jets, and Eagles) before finding himself out of the league just five years after getting drafted.

Tebow then announced he would pursue a career in professional baseball. After signing with the Mets organization, Tebow spent four years in New York's farm system without reaching the Major Leagues before he announced his retirement in 2021.

He made headlines once again when he announced the same year that he was attempting a comeback in the NFL. He signed with Jacksonville as a tight end but was ultimately cut during training camp.

Many people scoffed at Tebow for his persistence, but he never let the fear of failure keep him from pushing forward.

During Tebow's transition from football to baseball, ESPN's David Flemming wrote an article about Tebow's journey, titled, "Tim Tebow's Relentless Pursuit of Failure."

In the article, Flemming wrote, "In parting ways with the Patriots, Tebow tweeted 2 Corinthians 12:9, which says, in part, that 'power is perfected in weakness' and, therefore, the best way to have

Christ's power dwell inside you is by boasting of your weaknesses. This seems to be the moment where Tebow was able to meld his rapidly dwindling prospects as an NFL quarterback with the universal connection to, and the spiritual rewards of, failing with honor and purpose—sometimes over and over."[1]

We know Tebow's professional career was filled with disappointments, but what if God was doing something deeper within him? It's one thing when athletes give God praise and glory after a win, but Tebow pointed to God through his multiple failures.

Mark Anshel, author of *In Praise of Failure*, was quoted in Flemming's article saying, "If helping people deal with failure is how you believe you were called to serve God, then I'd say attempting to become a professional baseball player out of the blue at 29 is the absolute best place for him to be."

It's not something we want to believe, but what if God is leading us on a path that includes tremendous failure according to the world's standards?

What if our lives on earth aren't about revealing God's love and power through our wins and successes but through hardships and failures? Do we believe that God's glory and goodness are on full display when we are weak?

What if a place of failure is exactly where we need to be to surrender to Jesus?

Failure is at the core of the gospel because our failing reflects our need. We fail in our efforts at being "good enough" to earn salvation on our own, and that's why we rely on Jesus.

Ephesians 2:8–9 says, "God saved you by his grace when you believed. And you can't take credit for this; it is a gift from God. Salvation is not a reward for the good things we have done, so none of us can boast about it."

---

1. David Flemming, "Tim Tebow's Relentless Pursuit of Failure," ESPN, March 1, 2017, https://www.espn.com/mlb/story/_/id/18791367/tim-tebow-relentless-pursuit-failure.

Let's view failure in a different light and recognize that God can be found in the middle of it. Salvation, purpose, and strength are available in our weakness.

I'm Bryce Johnson, and you can *UNPACK* that!

PRAYER: *Heavenly Father, I'm blown away at how You use failure in my life to draw me closer to You and deepen my dependence on You. I need Your grace and strength in my weakness, and I trust You to mightily work in my broken-ness. I believe there is a purpose in my failure, and I pray You would help me see it. I pray this in Jesus' name. Amen.*

How has failure grown you and changed you for the better?

How would viewing failure differently change your perspective on stepping out in faith?

DID YOU KNOW

Did you know Tim Tebow holds the NCAA record for most consecutive games in which he both threw for a touchdown and rushed for a touchdown with 14?

My Own Game Film

Every week in the NFL, coaches and players watch game film to see what was done well on the field and what aspects of their play need improvement. They also spend time watching game film of their upcoming opponent to figure out ways to stop them and come up with offensive plays to combat the defense.

What's interesting, however, is that the best teams seem to spend more time and energy working on themselves than on thinking about what the other teams might do. If a team focuses on improving its offensive line and opening up more holes for its running back, the opponent won't matter as much.

Teams can't control what their opponent will do, but they do have the ability to practice and make the necessary changes in their own locker rooms. It's not that a team doesn't prepare for their competition, but it comes down to having a mentality that insists, "We have to take care of *our* business first" and make the necessary adjustments.

So many bad teams spend their time complaining about the refs or making excuses that they don't properly point the finger at themselves. They get caught up in what the media is saying about them or how they compare to other teams in their division.

It serves teams better to evaluate their own weekly play on the field and figure out improvements they can make instead of worrying so much about what other teams are doing.

When it comes to our own lives, we have a similar choice to make. Do we focus on our own skills, work, calling, responsibilities, growth, and improvement . . . or do we spend all our time worrying about how we compare to others? Are we more concerned with what others are doing and how we don't stack up . . . or are we content with examining our own lives and being obedient to what God is asking of us individually?

Of course, I'm not saying we don't care for others, serve others, or think more about others than we do ourselves. But when it comes to improvement and obedience, we need to take personal responsibility first. We don't want to get caught up in comparing or blaming.

Galatians 6:4–5 says, "Pay careful attention to your own work, for then you will get the satisfaction of a job well done, and you won't need to compare yourself to anyone else. For we are each responsible for our own conduct."

The Amplified Version of the same verses put it this way: "But each one must carefully scrutinize his own work [examining his actions, attitudes, and behavior], and then he can have the personal satisfaction and inner joy of doing something commendable without comparing himself to another. For every person will have to bear [with patience] his own burden [of faults and shortcomings for which he alone is responsible]."

Also, when we seek Jesus and follow His Word, we are daily changed from the inside out. By making the proper personal adjustments, we become more equipped to handle the enemy or our opponent.

Let's evaluate our own hearts and scrutinize our own "game film" as we submit to God's transforming power.

I'm Bryce Johnson, and you can *UNPACK* that!

PRAYER: *Heavenly Father, I desire to always grow in my understanding of You and my devotion to You. Please change me and enhance my abilities to do Your work. I pray I won't be so worried about comparing or concerned with what everyone else is doing. I know I'm responsible for being a good steward of the life You've given me. In Jesus' name I pray. Amen.*

What do you struggle with the most when it comes to comparing?

Why do you think it's more important for a team to improve their own play first, and how do you think that parallels your own approach to life?

DID YOU KNOW

Did you know that former NFL linebacker Ray Lewis once built an entire room in his house dedicated to watching film after having a conversation with Peyton Manning's wife?

The Daily Rematch

O ne of the things I love about the NFL Playoffs is watching rematches of games played earlier in the season.

Since teams find themselves in a familiar situation, it's always intriguing to see how they will make adjustments after matching up against a team for the second or third time in the same year. Do they stick with a game plan they used previously, or do they come up with something new to hopefully throw their opponent off?

Regardless of the team's approach, we can always expect rematches to be intense contests. Despite the outcome of the last matchup, teams have to play well in the next game if they want to advance.

When it comes to our own lives, each day we face spiritual rematches of the battles we faced the day before. Galatians 5:17 tells us, "For the sinful nature has its desire which is opposed to the Spirit, and the [desire of the] Spirit opposes the sinful nature; for these [two, the sinful nature and the Spirit] are in direct opposition to each other [continually in conflict], so that you [as believers] do not [always] do whatever [good things] you want to do" (AMP).

Our enemy knows how to take us down, and he'll scheme against us based on our weaknesses.

That's why we must "be strong in the Lord and in the strength of his might. Put on the whole armor of God, that you may be able to stand against the schemes of the devil" (Ephesians 6:10–11 ESV).

Since it's a daily rematch, we must remember that whether we won or lost yesterday, today is a new fight. That means we can't let our pride mislead us into thinking we won't give in to sin today just because we "won" previously . . . or let our shame mislead us into thinking it's inevitable we'll fall again today because we did last time.

Rather, each day we acknowledge it's another battle. We must yield to the Holy Spirit when temptations come, and trust in God's strength to win the daily struggles we face.

Ephesians 6:12–17 says:

> For our struggle is not against flesh and blood, but against the rulers, against the authorities, against the cosmic powers of this darkness, against evil, spiritual forces in the heavens. For this reason take up the full armor of God, so that you may be able to resist in the evil day, and having prepared everything, to take your stand. Stand, therefore, with truth like a belt around your waist, righteousness like armor on your chest, and your feet sandaled with readiness for the gospel of peace. In every situation take up the shield of faith with which you can extinguish all the flaming arrows of the evil one. Take the helmet of salvation and the sword of the Spirit—which is the word of God. (CSB)

As we enter each day knowing a rematch is in store, we can still learn from our previous wins and losses while we rely on the full armor of God. Even though the spiritual battle continues each day during our time on earth, let's remember our eternal victory is secure when we surrender to Jesus and place our faith in Him.

I'm Bryce Johnson, and you can *UNPACK* that!

PRAYER: *Heavenly Father, I know I can't battle against my flesh and the evil that I'm up against on my own. I need You and Your power every day and ask You to help me remain humble and dependent on You to fight against temptation and the sin that's all around me. In Jesus' name I pray. Amen.*

What are the previous sins God has allowed you to overcome that you still have to battle each day with humility and His strength?

Why is it so important to understand that each day is a rematch and prepare accordingly to battle well spiritually?

 **DID YOU KNOW**

Did you know the Green Bay Packers and Chicago Bears share the record for most NFL games played against a single opponent, having faced off against each other more than 200 times?

Oral Roberts' Head Coach Explains His Job

In 2019, one of the main headlines during the NCAA Tournament was 15-seed Oral Roberts University knocking off Ohio State and Florida on its way to the Sweet 16. At the time, they were just the second team to ever reach that far as a 15-seed.

During his team's surprising run, Oral Roberts head coach Paul Mills discussed his mentality as a coach during an interview with SiriusXM: "It's not my job to fill player's cups. When we get done with practice, whether they receive anything I'm saying or not, I can't make them receive anything that I'm even talking about. My job is to empty mine, it's not to fill theirs. And you hope over the course of time that you're able to fill their cup, but it's not my job to fill their cup, it's my job to empty mine . . . so what I do every day, is ask myself, did I empty my cup, did I invest in those guys, did those guys know that I love them?"[1]

This makes a lot of sense. By doing what he could for his players, he emptied himself and gave all he had to them. As a result, he saw the fruit of being one of the last sixteen teams in the NCAA Tournament.

---

1.   Coach Mills ,on "College Sports on Sirius XM" (@SXMCollege), X (formerly known as Twitter), March 20, 2021, 11:26 a.m., https://twitter.com/SXMCollege/status/1373310077193568257.

What if we could adopt this process of emptying our own cups? What if, instead of being so full of ourselves, we humbly gave our lives in service to God and others?

By emptying our cups and investing in our spouses, kids, friends, neighbors, and coworkers, we can have a fruitful life. When we share the love of God, tell people the good news of Jesus, and pour ourselves out for others, the investment is always worthwhile—even if they don't receive it.

As Coach Mills explained, it's our responsibility to empty our own cups and let people know we love them. When we keep doing that, hopefully we'll be able to fill their cups over time.

Jesus is the perfect example of what it means to be poured out as a sacrifice for others. He laid down His life for us on the cross to save us from our sin.

Philippians 2:7 tells us, "He emptied Himself by assuming the form of a servant, taking on the likeness of humanity" (CSB).

Ephesians 5:1–2 says, "Therefore be imitators of God, as beloved children. And walk in love, as Christ loved us and gave himself up for us, a fragrant offering and sacrifice to God" (ESV).

First John 3:16 (AMP) explains, "By this we know [and have come to understand the depth and essence of His precious] love: that He [willingly] laid down His life for us [because He loved us]. And we ought to lay down our lives for the believers."

As we follow Jesus, we, in turn, empty and pour out ourselves. At the same time, we're filled by Him because He pours into us.

Let's be challenged by the words of Coach Mills: "It's not my job to fill their cup, it's my job to empty mine."

Let's remember to ask ourselves these questions: Did I empty my cup? Did I invest in others? Did they know that I love them?

I'm Bryce Johnson, and you can *UNPACK* that!

PRAYER: *Heavenly Father, I pray that I won't be full of myself, but instead I will empty my cup and lay down my life and my selfish desires to be a living sacrifice that is holy and pleasing to You. Please help me to pour myself out in service and love to others. In Jesus' name I pray. Amen.*

What holds you back from emptying your cup?

What do you think about Coach Mills' perspective on his job not being to fill his team's cup, but rather, to empty his?

DID YOU KNOW

Did you know only one 15-seed in history has advanced to the Elite Eight: Saint Peter's in 2022?

DAY FIFTEEN

When Stubbornness
Is Good

O f the four NBA championships the Golden State Warriors won between 2015 and 2022, none was more special than their 2022 title.

Many people doubted that, having suffered through multiple years of injuries, key departures, and aging stars, the team could win another championship with its core group of players. However, the Warriors refused to back down and never stopped believing they would win again.

On TheAthletic.com, NBA writer David Aldridge wrote in an article following the team's 2022 title, "Hall of Famer Chris Webber has this great saying about championship teams. Often, they aren't the most talented or the best coached. They just, usually, are the most stubborn."[1]

At first glance, the word "stubborn" has a negative connotation. Of course, being stubborn in the wrong way can be a major character flaw, but when used in the context of who the Warriors were, it's positive and fitting.

According to Merriam-Webster.com, synonyms for the word *stubborn* include "firm," "adamant," "persistent," "uncompromising," "unbending," and "tenacious."[2]

1. David Aldridge, "Warriors, Like All the Champions They Are, Refuse to Leave the Stage: 'We're Very Stubborn,'" *Athletic,* June 17, 2022, https://theathletic.com/3368175/2022/06/17/aldridge-the-warriors-like-all-champions-refuse-to-leave-the-stage.
2. Merriam-Webster, Merriam-Webster.com Thesaurus, s.v. "stubborn," accessed Janu-

Warriors forward Draymond Green said after winning the 2022 championship, "We're very stubborn and it has been tested. You go through injuries. You get punched in the mouth a couple times. And it takes an incredible amount of resilience and togetherness and trust in each other."[3]

The Warriors proved that adversity wasn't going to stop them from knowing who they were and what they needed to do. In the end, their stubbornness, persistence, and uncompromising belief were rewarded with another Larry O'Brien Trophy.

When it comes to our own lives as followers of Jesus, the right kind of stubbornness is also valuable and rewarding. When we face adversity, we want to remain firm, resolute, tenacious, resilient, and persistent.

James 1:12 tells us, "Blessed is the man who remains steadfast under trial, for when he has stood the test he will receive the crown of life, which God has promised to those who love him" (ESV).

During the seasons of our lives when difficulties seem to be hitting us in every direction, we want to be "stubborn" by consistently doing the right things and never giving up.

Galatians 6:9 provides this encouragement: "Let us not grow weary of doing good, for in due season we will reap, if we do not give up" (ESV).

We must also remain stubborn when the world tries to take us off course or attack our faith.

First Corinthians 16:13 warns, "Be on guard; stand firm in your faith [in God, respecting His precepts and keeping your doctrine sound]. Act like [mature] men and be courageous; be strong" (AMP).

If persecution, criticism, or temptation comes our way, we must stubbornly refuse to back down or stop believing the truth of the gospel of Jesus Christ.

ary 6, 2024, https://www.merriam-webster.com/thesaurus/stubborn.

3.   David Aldridge, "Warriors, Like the Champions They Are, Refuse to Leave the Stage.

We don't have to let our opponent cause us to waver from knowing who we are in Christ and what He's calling us to do. We must stand firm in our faith, remaining stubborn in our hope of victory.

Hebrews 10:23 says, "Let us hold tightly without wavering to the hope we affirm, for God can be trusted to keep His promise."

Let's learn from championship teams that we don't have to be the most talented—just the most stubborn!

I'm Bryce Johnson, and you can *UNPACK* that!

PRAYER: *Heavenly Father, I'm confident in Your truth and Your promises, but please help me to have a faith that's strong and immovable. When I go through adversity, show me how to be steadfast, uncompromising, and resilient. I pray that my faith won't waver because my hope is in You. Thank you for helping me to stand firm and never give up. In Jesus' name I pray. Amen.*

When have you demonstrated the right kind of stubbornness and persistence through adversity?

In what situations is it toughest for you to stand firm and be stubborn?

DID YOU KNOW

Did you know that Stephen Curry holds the NBA record for most career three-pointers made?

DAY SIXTEEN

Victims of Our Own Success

The 2018–2019 Tampa Bay Lightning was one of the best teams to ever take the ice. The Lightning scored goals at an incredible rate and finished the regular season with 62 wins, tying for the most in NHL history.

Coasting its way through the regular season, the team had high hopes for the playoffs. However, things changed quickly when the Lightning were surprisingly swept out of the playoffs in the first round by the Columbus Blue Jackets.

As shocked as everyone was because of Tampa Bay's playoff exit, Lightning head coach Jon Cooper said this after his team's loss in Game 4: "When you have the amount of points we had, it's a blessing and a curse, in a way. You don't play any meaningful hockey for a long time. Then all of a sudden you have to ramp it up. It's not an excuse, it's reality."[1]

ESPN.com writer Greg Wyshynski, summed it up this way: "They were victims of their own success."[2]

It's a fair perspective when considering that all their wins during the regular season didn't equate to success when it mattered most.

1. Greg Wyshynski, "Anatomy of a Playoff Collapse: What Happened to the Tampa Bay Lightning?," ESPN, April 17, 2019, https://www.espn.com/nhl/story/_/id/26540856/anatomy-playoff-collapse-happened-tampa-bay-lightning.

2. Greg Wyshynski, "Cooper: Ousted Lightning Victims of Own Success," ESPN, April 17, 2019, https://www.espn.com/nhl/story/_/id/26542145/ousted-lightning-victims-own-success.

Unfortunately, this concept of being victims of our own success translates to our own lives as well. When we're experiencing big wins, it's easy to get caught up in ourselves. We often get complacent and believe the lie that we no longer need to depend on God.

Of course, winning in the regular season doesn't have to lead to defeat in the playoffs, just as having success in life doesn't have to have a negative result. But getting tripped up when we're rolling right along is a real possibility for us all.

The Bible gives us the story of the rich young ruler who asked Jesus about obtaining eternal life. When Jesus told him that he needed to keep the commandments,

> the young man said to Him, "I have kept all these things [from my youth]; what do I still lack?" Jesus answered him, "If you wish to be perfect [that is, have the spiritual maturity that accompanies godly character with no moral or ethical deficiencies], go and sell what you have and give [the money] to the poor, and you will have treasure in heaven; and come, follow Me [becoming My disciple, believing and trusting in Me and walking the same path of life that I walk]." But when the young man heard this, he left grieving and distressed, for he owned much property and had many possessions [which he treasured more than his relationship with God]. (Matthew 19:16–22 AMP)

This rich young ruler was a victim of his own success. He was not able to part with his money and fully surrender his life to Jesus. Instead, he allowed his success to trap him and get him caught up in the life he had built for himself.

Let's ask ourselves if we are victims of our own success and if something is getting in the way of the victory that really matters.

Let's not get caught up in our regular season success or cling to worldly treasures but accept Jesus' invitation to experience a meaningful and eternal life with Him.

I'm Bryce Johnson, and you can *UNPACK* that!

PRAYER: *Heavenly Father, thank You for saving me and allowing me to join You one day in heaven. I pray that I won't value anything more than Jesus and that I won't be trapped by worldly success. I desire to live a life of meaning. In Jesus' name I pray. Amen.*

In what season of life have you experienced worldly success, and how did it affect you spiritually?

What does it look like to experience winning from a spiritual standpoint regardless of whether you're having worldly success?

DID YOU KNOW

Did you know the NHL record for most points by a team in a regular season is 135, set by the Boston Bruins in 2022-2023?

I Don't Know

I consider myself knowledgeable about the NFL since I keep up with the games, players, and stories all season long. Heading into any season, I have my predictions and expectations of what will happen. Then, once the season begins, I quickly realize that I have no clue.

Most football fans, just like me, pretend to be expert NFL prognosticators and want their opinions to be proven as facts. But the truth is, we just don't know. We don't know why coaches do certain things, why teams play so inconsistently, and how the season is going to play out.

We don't know what's really going on with players behind the scenes or how injured they truly are. We are limited and don't have all the facts.

When it comes to life, we also like to have all the answers, pretend we're all-knowing, and claim to have everything figured out as to what should happen. It's tough to admit we just don't know.

We like to make predictions about what we're going to do and when we're going to do it, and have strong opinions about what's best.

However, James 4:13–16 warns us, "Look here, you who say, 'Today or tomorrow we are going to a certain town and will stay there a year. We will do business there and make a profit.' How do you know what your life will be like tomorrow? Your life is like the morning fog—it's here a little while, then it's gone. What you ought to say is, 'If the Lord wants us to, we will live and do this or that.' Otherwise, you are boasting about your own pretentious plans, and all such boasting is evil."

We must remain humble about what we're going to do and what to expect in the future. We don't know the blessings up ahead or the struggles awaiting us. It requires humility to willingly admit that we just don't know.

We don't know what God's perfect timing will be, how He's going to work out our situation for good, or how He's going to use it for His purposes.

We don't know how we're going to get through a tough season, and we don't know why God allows certain things to happen.

We don't know when He's going to open unexpected doors. We don't understand why certain things are taking place and why God hasn't revealed the answers we've been waiting for.

Romans 11:33 declares, "Oh, how great are God's riches and wisdom and knowledge! How impossible it is for us to understand his decisions and his ways!"

We don't always know what God is up to or how things are going to play out. Yes, God reveals so much to us in His Word, and we gain knowledge and wisdom as we seek Him. But even so, we have a limited understanding of elements beyond our control.

Guess what: that's okay because we serve a God who knows what He's doing, and we just need to trust Him! We need to accept that although we don't have all the answers, He does, and He guides us each step of the way.

Let's remember that He's with us, He loves us, and He's faithful, so we can "trust in the Lord with all [our hearts], and do not lean on [our] own understanding." This passage further instructs us, "In all your ways acknowledge him, and he will make straight your paths.

Be not wise in your own eyes; fear the Lord, and turn away from evil" (Proverbs 3:5–7 ESV).

I'm Bryce Johnson, and you can *UNPACK* that!

PRAYER: *Heavenly Father, there is so much about life and the future that I just don't know. Help me to be okay with that as I'm reminded that You're in control and are worthy to be trusted. Please show me the way to go and help me remain humble and open-handed to whatever plans You have for me. In Jesus' name I pray. Amen.*

What situations are you facing today where you need to admit you just don't know what's going to happen and that you need to trust God?

How does acknowledging your limited understanding give you peace as you trust in God?

DID YOU KNOW

Did you know that for seven consecutive years, ESPN broadcaster Chris Berman wrongly predicted at the start of the season that the San Francisco 49ers and the Buffalo Bills would meet in the Super Bowl?

Responding to the Pressure

I t's a joy to watch the Masters Tournament, with all its intriguing stories and incredible players. But what jumps out to me is the atmosphere of pressure that permeates this revered golf tournament.

There's no denying that every golfer feels some level of pressure when showing up in Augusta.

With more eyes on the players during the Masters, there's heightened intensity and, with the allure of the tournament, there's also a stronger desire to win.

Every golfer who steps foot on the course is fighting an emotional and mental battle not to let the pressure negatively affect his game. Those who thrive under pressure and play free and light are the ones who find themselves in a position to win.

The course is challenging, and the competition is fierce, but the players who have the right mentality, understand how to deal with the pressure, know how to overcome bad shots, and play with ease are the ones who win. They still have the pressure, yet it doesn't lead them to be overwhelmed.

Most of us aren't attempting to sink a putt with the world watching, but every day we wake up with pressure and burdens. We feel the weight of responsibility at work, as parents, as spouses, and as people living in a broken world.

There's no denying that pressure is unavoidable, so instead of pretending it's not there, we need to embrace it and deal with it properly.

What if instead of being stressed-out, we thrived under pressure and were the ones who lived free and light, finding ourselves in a position to win?

Thankfully, Jesus took the ultimate pressure off us by dying on our behalf, taking on the burden of sin, and rising again. We don't have to feel the pressure of earning salvation based on our own merits. Jesus offers us His gift of grace and invites us to follow Him and be committed to His way.

Jesus tells us in Matthew 11:28–30, "Come to Me, all who are weary and heavily burdened [by religious rituals that provide no peace], and I will give you rest [refreshing your souls with salvation]. Take My yoke upon you and learn from Me [following Me as My disciple], for I am gentle and humble in heart, and you will find rest (renewal, blessed quiet) for your souls. For My yoke is easy [to bear] and My burden is light" (AMP).

John Mark Comer, in his book *The Ruthless Elimination of Hurry*, writes, "[Jesus] offers his apprentices a whole new way to bear the weight of our humanity: with ease. At his side. Like two oxen in a field, tied shoulder to shoulder. With Jesus doing all the heavy lifting."[1]

Life is hard, but those who rely on Jesus are the ones who win. We have the right understanding of how to deal with the pressure and live in peace because He's right there with us.

Since we are connected to Him, He's available to carry our burdens and bear the weight so we can live life free and light with Him.

---

1. John Mark Comer, *The Ruthless Elimination of Hurry: How to Stay Emotionally Healthy and Spiritually Alive in the Chaos of the Modern World* (New York: Waterbrook, 2019), 88.

He strengthens us, empowers us, and helps us overcome whatever is attempting to weigh us down.

I'm Bryce Johnson, and you can *UNPACK* that!

PRAYER: *Heavenly Father, I know life is hard and pressures and burdens are always attempting to weigh me down. I pray I'll take Jesus up on His invitation to live His way and with Him carrying the load and stop trying to do things in my own strength. In Jesus' name I pray. Amen.*

What pressures and burdens tend to weigh you down?

What changes should you make so you can live with the ease of knowing Jesus is willing to carry the weight?

 **DID YOU KNOW**

Did you know that the lowest winning score at the Masters is 20-under-par (268), set by Dustin Johnson in 2020?

"Look, Losing Is Our Best Option"

We all know that sports are driven by winning (and making money, of course), as players go out each game to compete and contribute to what they hope is a victory.

Everything a team does—from off-season training to putting together elaborate game plans to coaches making adjustments during time-outs—is intended to put the team in the best position to win.

With the point of the game being to win, the concept of "tanking," or purposely losing by not doing everything you can to give your team the best chance to win, goes against the grain. The process doesn't seem right, and it's difficult for fans to accept.

Even so, tanking in the NBA has become a strategy that teams have implemented to increase their chances of winning the draft lottery. They believe they can rebuild their rosters through the draft and want to have the best pick possible. This simply means the more losing they do right now, the better chance they have of winning in the future.

But the NBA doesn't encourage use of this plan, and Dallas Mavericks owner Mark Cuban once got in trouble for admitting that his team was embracing their losses. In an interview with Julius Erving on the *House Call with Dr. J* podcast, Cuban said, "I'm probably not supposed to say this, but, like, I just had dinner with a bunch of our guys the other night, and here we are, you know, we weren't competing for the playoffs. I was like, 'Look, losing is our best option.'"[1]

Their losing led to having the fifth pick in the draft, which allowed them to pick Trae Young and then trade him to the Hawks for Luka Dončić. Although it might not make sense at first glance or it's hard for those associated with the NBA to promote, the principle of "losing is our best option" can be true for certain teams.

When it comes to our own lives, it's a core principle that's always true and one we must be willing to embrace as followers of Jesus. Mark 8:34–35 says, "And calling the crowd to him with his disciples, [Jesus] said to them, 'If anyone would come after me, let him deny himself and take up his cross and follow me. For whoever would save his life will lose it, but whoever loses his life for my sake and the gospel's will save it'" (ESV).

This challenge goes against the grain because we live in a society that's all about winning with worldly success, personal gain, and self-satisfaction. We're expected to acquire as much fame, money, material possessions, and power as we can.

However, following Jesus requires us to change our approach to winning. Our mindset shifts from trying to win "this season," to being focused on eternity and the victory found in the cross.

When we're willing to lose worldly pursuits and the trappings of sin and say to ourselves, "Look, losing is our best option," we gain Jesus and the abundant life we're meant to live.

In Matthew 10:38–39, Jesus also tells us, "Whoever does not take his cross and follow me is not worthy of me. Whoever finds

---

1.   SportsDay Staff, "Mavericks Owner Mark Cuban Admits to Telling Players Tanking Is Best Option, *Dallas Morning News,* February 19, 2018, https://www.dallasnews.com/sports/mavericks/2018/02/20/mavericks-owner-mark-cuban-admits-to-telling-players-tanking-is-best-option.

his life will lose it, and whoever loses his life for my sake will find it" (ESV).

Let's make every effort to "lose" the things that hold us back in our walk with God. Let's deny ourselves, take up our crosses, and follow the One who gave up everything so we could spend eternity with Him.

I'm Bryce Johnson, and you can *UNPACK* that!

PRAYER: *Heavenly Father, please show me what I need to lose and let go of to live the life available to me. Please help me take up my cross each day and follow You. I pray that I won't cling to the things of this world but rather cling to the hope found in Jesus. In His name I pray. Amen.*

In what ways is it most difficult for you to embrace losing the things of this world?

What does it look like for you to take up your cross each day and follow Jesus?

DID YOU KNOW

Did you know the Philadelphia 76ers set the record for most losses in a regular season, dropping 73 contests during the 1972-1973 season?

Do You Always Want to Win?

T he NFL preseason is always filled with captivating story-lines as young players fight for roster spots and veterans try to prove they still belong as the starter.

The preseason is designed to get players warmed up for the regular season while giving coaches a chance to evaluate which players belong on their team and how the depth chart should take shape.

Since the preseason doesn't officially count toward a team's record, winning these games isn't a top priority for most coaches. They're glad if their team happens to win, but not incredibly concerned if they don't. These are just exhibition games, and the desire to win isn't very strong for most.

However, the Baltimore Ravens have taken a different approach over the years, as they achieved the NFL record for most consecutive preseason wins at 24. Even though many people discredit what the Ravens accomplished in the preseason by saying that the games don't matter, I love how it demonstrates a winning culture and shows that winning is always important to the team.

Every time the Ravens step on the field (regardless of who is playing or what part of the season it is), they want to win, and they expect to win.

Recognizing how the Ravens value winning, what if we drop the "it's just preseason" attitude when doing seemingly mundane tasks and embrace a winning mentality in our lives? As followers of Jesus, we must stop acting as though supposed meaningless things don't matter when, in reality, they matter a great deal.

What if instead of downplaying certain activities or situations, we approached all of them with a consistent winning attitude, so that everything we do and how we do it matters and has the potential to bring God the most glory?

First Corinthians 10:31 tells us, "Whether you eat or drink, or whatever you do, do it all for the glory of God." What if we did everything to please, honor, and make much of God?

What if we never turned off our passion for evangelism and winning people to Christ?

What if we approached the ordinary tasks of life with an extraordinary attitude that sets us apart from the world?

What if we viewed every time we stepped "on the field" as an opportunity to serve Jesus and point people to Him?

Colossians 3:17 says, "Whatever you do [no matter what it is] in word or deed, do everything in the name of the Lord Jesus [and in dependence on Him], giving thanks to God the Father through Him" (AMP).

Let's embrace a "winning culture" that approaches life through the lens of eternity, desires to bring God glory in everything we do, and knows that nothing we do for Him is ever "just a meaningless preseason game."

Let's focus on this life-changing challenge in Colossians 3:23–24: "Whatever you do [whatever your task may be], work from the soul [that is, put in your very best effort], as [something done] for the Lord and not for men, knowing [with all certainty] that it is from the Lord [not from men] that you will receive the inheritance which is your [greatest] reward. It is the Lord Christ whom you [actually] serve" (AMP).

I'm Bryce Johnson, and you can *UNPACK* that!

PRAYER: *Heavenly Father, please teach me to view every day as a chance to serve You and bring You glory. Help me not to downplay certain situations or tasks, but instead do everything in Your name as I work from the soul. I pray my life will be marked by a winning attitude that is rooted in living for Your glory. In Jesus' name I pray. Amen.*

In what areas of your life do you need to have a winning attitude and approach?

What is something in your life that you've downplayed or not taken seriously that you could do in a way that brings God glory?

DID YOU KNOW

Did you know only two teams in history have won the Super Bowl after going undefeated in the preseason: the 2003 New England Patriots and the 2013 Seattle Seahawks?

Name, Image, and Likeness

College sports changed forever after the door swung open for college athletes to profit from their names, images, and likenesses. Since the NCAA changed its legislation, college athletes have made significant money through sponsorships, product endorsements, autographs, and appearances. This has led to college athletes being seen in commercials, staying longer in school, and benefiting financially from their social media platforms.

There are plenty of gray areas and unintended consequences that have taken place as well, but there seem to be endless opportunities for athletes to take full advantage of promoting their names, images, and likenesses, or "NILs."

Athletes are quickly recognizing the value of their NILs. They can now embrace their power, the added freedom, the enjoyable benefits, and the potential for financial transformation.

An interesting parallel to name, image, and likeness found in the Bible shows how our lives can be transformed when we understand God's "NIL."

First, we must embrace the truth that God is the Creator. His approach to making humans is found in Genesis 1:26–27: "Then God said, 'Let us make man in our image, after our likeness. And let them have dominion over the fish of the sea and over the birds of the heavens and over the livestock and over all the earth and over every creeping thing that creeps on the earth.' So God created man in his own image, in the image of God he created him; male and female he created them" (ESV).

We are made in the image of God and after His likeness, but because of sin and brokenness, we need to be born again. This happens by placing our faith in the death and resurrection of Jesus Christ and receiving His salvation and repenting of our sin.

In Christ, we are made new. Ephesians 4:24 tells us to "to put on the new self, created after the likeness of God in true righteousness and holiness" (ESV). Colossians 3:10 explains that Christians "have put on the new self, which is being renewed in knowledge after the image of its creator" (ESV).

As we follow Jesus, we become more like Him and are transformed into His image.

Second Corinthians 3:16–18 says, "Whenever someone turns to the Lord, the veil is taken away. For the Lord is the Spirit, and wherever the Spirit of the Lord is, there is freedom. So all of us who have had that veil removed can see and reflect the glory of the Lord. And the Lord—who is the Spirit—makes us more and more like him as we are changed into his glorious image."

The Lord's image and likeness are available to us in Jesus, and there is also power in His name.

Romans 10:13 declares that "everyone who calls on the name of the Lord will be saved.'" Philippians 2:9–11 adds, "God has highly exalted [Jesus] and bestowed on him the name that is above every name, so that at the name of Jesus every knee should bow, in heaven and on earth and under the earth, and every tongue confess that Jesus Christ is Lord, to the glory of God the Father" (ESV).

We recognize that there is some earthly value in the names, images, and likenesses of athletes. But ultimately, we find eternal value in the name of our Creator, Savior, and Lord. Praise God that we can be conformed to His image and likeness!

I'm Bryce Johnson, and you can *UNPACK* that!

PRAYER: *Heavenly Father, I believe in the power and freedom found in the name of Jesus. Thank You for conforming me to the image of Your Son and transforming me into Your likeness. I pray I will represent Your name, image, and likeness well as I live my life for Your glory. In Jesus' name I pray. Amen.*

What comes to mind when you think about the name of Jesus?

In what ways has He transformed you into His likeness?

DID YOU KNOW

Did you know that college athletes earned an estimated $917 million in the first year that NIL was made legal?

DAY TWENTY-TWO

Oh, Come On

Dallas Mavericks star Luka Dončić is undeniably one of the best players in the NBA. Yet, as impactful as Dončić is on the floor, he sometimes has a tough time controlling his emotions and frustrations.

After receiving just five technical fouls in his rookie season, Dončić has finished in the top seven in the league for most technicals for multiple seasons since. He understands he has some work to do so the technicals don't become an ongoing issue.

During a TNT interview following a team win, he acknowledged, "I'm complaining way too much, and I've gotta work on that. I just have to stay calm and not talk to them [refs], I have to learn from that."[1]

As we know, Dončić isn't the only superstar to struggle with this, and sports have a culture of complaining. Whether it's the players, the coaches, or the fans, someone is always finding something to complain about.

We can all admit that in sports and in life, our response is all too often to complain or say, "Oh, come on" when any of the following situations arise:

- something doesn't go our way
- we don't get what we want

1.   Jasmyn Wimbish, Mavericks' Luka Doncic Admits He Has to Stop 'Complaining Way Too Much' to Referees," CBS Sports, May 7, 2021, https://www.cbssports.com/nba/news/mavericks-luka-doncic-admits-he-has-to-stop-complaining-way-too-much-to-referees/.

- we don't agree with authority
- a "call" doesn't benefit us
- someone else gets something we wish we had
- someone doesn't do something the way we think they should
- we have to wait for something
- someone doesn't do what we want them to do

The last one especially hits home because we're guilty of saying, "Oh, come on!" to God when He doesn't answer our prayers the way we think He should.

When things don't go exactly how we want them to, what if we change our approach and acknowledge, as Luka did, "I'm complaining way too much, and I've gotta work on that"? After all, the Bible does say, "Do everything without complaining and arguing, so that no one can criticize you. Live clean, innocent lives as children of God, shining like bright lights in a world full of crooked and perverse people" (Philippians 2:14–15).

By being thankful, remembering God's past faithfulness, and acknowledging how good He is right now, we can combat our impulse to complain about both silly things and more serious challenges alike.

The Bible says to "give thanks in all circumstances; for this is the will of God in Christ Jesus for you" (1 Thessalonians 5:18 ESV).

We also have to choose joy instead of allowing inconveniences, "bad calls," or unfortunate situations to steal our joy and leave us focused on our complaints.

When we're aware of God's presence and view our lives with an eternal perspective, we realize that many of the things we complain about are meaningless and inconsequential. We even become eager to "move on to the next play."

Ultimately, God is so gracious and kind to us. Instead of complaining when He doesn't do things our way, we should say to *our-*

selves as we're about to complain to the One who gives us everything, "Oh, come on!"

Let's humble ourselves before God and be thankful not only for each breath and blessing but for His love and grace that allow us to know Him. May our voices declare praises instead of complaints!

I'm Bryce Johnson, and you can *UNPACK* that!

PRAYER: *Heavenly Father, forgive me for my complaining, and please help me have a better response and perspective when my circumstances are tough. I ask that You bring to mind everything I need to be thankful for and give me the strength to resist the urge to complain when things don't appear to go my way. I desire to live with joy and hope, resting in Your grace and goodness. In Jesus' name I pray. Amen.*

What do you find yourself complaining about the most?

Why do you think you complain about certain things?

DID YOU KNOW

Did you know that the NBA record for most career technical fouls is 332, set by Karl Malone?

The Powerful Pregame Speech

Trailing the St. Louis Blues three games to two in the 2019 Stanley Cup Finals, the Boston Bruins responded with an impressive 5–1 victory in game 6 to force a winner-take-all final contest.

In the aftermath of the victory, many Bruins players pointed to a pregame speech by alternate captain Patrice Bergeron for having set the tone and igniting them.

Matt Porter from the *Boston Globe* wrote in his article, "One of the greatest Bruins poured his heart onto the floor in front of his teammates, with the Stanley Cup in the building, as they prepared to keep their season alive. Bergeron didn't produce a point in Boston's 5–1 trouncing of St. Louis in Game 6 Sunday, but his teammates turned his words into furious action, playing their best game of the series at the most critical time."[1]

Left winger Jake DeBrusk said, "It made us all want to run through a wall." Defenseman Charlie McAvoy added, "It was exactly what we needed, and he stepped up. When he talks, you listen."[2]

We've seen great inspirational speeches in sports movies or heard about others like Bergeron's, and we know that for a team

---

1. Matt Porter, "Patrice Bergeron Lit a Fire with His Pregame Speech, and the Bruins Forced a Game 7," *Boston Globe,* June 10, 2019, https://www.bostonglobe.com/sports/bruins/2019/06/09/bruins/2M7wep2mdWtydra1QRaFsL/story.html.
2. Porter, "Patrice Bergeron Lit a Fire."

to respond to the words, they must respect and believe in the one speaking.

I doubt many of us hear "pregame speeches" in our everyday lives, but what if we viewed Jesus' words that way?

When He talks, do we listen? Do His teachings, sayings, and "pregame speeches" cause us to turn His words into "furious action"? Do we respect and believe in what He says so much that we respond to His words? Are we willing to run through a wall for Him, so to speak?

Bergeron "poured his heart onto the floor in front of his teammates" and his teammates greatly responded. Jesus, on the other hand, poured out His very life, making the ultimate sacrifice by dying on the cross for us. He then inspired His disciples with a call to action, and they enthusiastically responded.

The "pregame speeches" Jesus gave while He walked the earth still ring true for us today. He gives us clear instructions in the Bible, so when He talks, do we listen?

Let's be challenged to hear the following verses as parts of a "pregame speech" and allow Jesus' words to inspire us to live for Him and go out into this world and truly give all we have:

> "Whoever wants to be my disciple must deny themselves and take up their cross and follow me." (Matthew 16:24 NIV)

> "Seek first [God's] kingdom and his righteousness, and all these things will be given to you as well." (Matthew 6:33 NIV)

> "'Love the Lord your God with all your heart and with all your soul and with all your mind.' This is the first and greatest commandment. And the second is like it: 'Love your neighbor as yourself.'" (Matthew 22:37–40 NIV)

"Go and make disciples of all nations, baptizing them in the name of the Father and of the Son and of the Holy Spirit." (Matthew 28:19 NIV)

"With man [salvation] is impossible, but with God all things are possible." (Matthew 19:26 NIV)

Let's go!! I'm Bryce Johnson, and you can *UNPACK* that!

PRAYER: *Heavenly Father, thank You for sending Jesus to pay my punishment on the cross. I'm also grateful for His words and the power behind them. Help me take to heart what He spoke and live with a strong passion to turn His words into action. Please give me the strength to do so. I pray this in His name. Amen.*

Which of these verses inspires and motivates you the most?

Which of these verses is the hardest to hear, read, and implement in your life?

 **DID YOU KNOW**

Did you know Patrice Bergeron has won the Selke Trophy, given to the NHL's best defensive forward, a record six times?

The NFL Is the Great Revealer

Former Heisman Trophy–winning quarterback Tim Tebow had an inspiring, disappointing, incredible, and highly polarizing career.

After a short stint in the NFL, a tenure as a broadcaster, and an attempt at a professional baseball career, Tebow decided to make a comeback attempt in the NFL at age thirty-three, trying out as a tight end for his former Florida coach, Urban Meyer.

When the news of his signing with the Jacksonville Jaguars was released, there were strong opinions and a plethora of predictions regarding the outcome.

There were also numerous questions swirling around:

Has he been out of the league too long?

Is he really going to block anyone as a tight end?

Will he be a distraction?

Can he make an impact on the team by switching positions?

During that time, Fox Sports radio hosts Doug Gottlieb and Charles Robinson, from Yahoo Sports, were questioning and wondering how things might turn out for Tebow. Robinson reminded everyone, "Oh, we'll find out. I mean that's the great thing about the NFL. It is the great revealer. This will not be left up to question. Whatever he's going to be, we will see very quickly. The NFL is the great revealer. We'll know pretty quickly what Tim Tebow is or isn't or can or can't be."[1]

Robinson was right. Once Tebow stepped onto the field and lined up at tight end, they were able to see he wasn't doing what an NFL tight end needs to do. He was exposed as not being able to block and catch passes at the level required of him.

It's true: a player can't hide for long, and the NFL may be the great revealer in terms of athleticism, talent, and skill. Yet, there's also a great revealer for us when it comes to our faith journey.

God's Word is our Great Revealer not only because it reveals His truth, His character, and His way, but also because it exposes, convicts, confirms, and shows us who we really are.

Hebrews 4:12–13 says, "The Word of God is alive and powerful. It is sharper than the sharpest two-edged sword, cutting between soul and spirit, between joint and marrow. It exposes our innermost thoughts and desires. Nothing in all creation is hidden from God. Everything is naked and exposed before his eyes, and he is the one to whom we are accountable."

The Living Bible (TLB) puts it this way: "For whatever God says to us is full of living power: it is sharper than the sharpest dagger, cutting swift and deep into our innermost thoughts and desires with all their parts, exposing us for what we really are. He knows about everyone, everywhere. Everything about us is bare and wide open to the all-seeing eyes of our living God; nothing can be hidden from him to whom we must explain all that we have done."

1. "Hr 3: Charles Robinson on the State of the Packers," May 11, 2021, in *The Doug Gottlieb Show*, produced by Omny Studios, podcast, https://omny.fm/shows/the-doug-gottlieb-show/hr-3-charles-robinson-on-the-state-of-the-packers.

When we read or hear God's Word, it shows us our brokenness and need for a Savior. We are fully exposed before God, and we are shown our true spiritual condition. It also brings to light the areas of our hearts we still need to surrender and align with Him, the sins we need to confess, and the aspects of our character that we need God to transform. The need for healing and restoration becomes evident, so we allow the power of God's Word to work in us.

As we realize God's Word is the "Great Revealer," let's place our hope in Jesus, choose to obey, and have hearts that desire after Him.

I'm Bryce Johnson, and you can *UNPACK* that!

PRAYER: *Heavenly Father, thank You so much for giving us Your Word. I pray it will transform my heart. I ask that my faith will be revealed as genuine and my desires will align with Yours. In Jesus' name I pray. Amen.*

How has God's Word made a difference in your life?

How has God used His Word to expose sin in your life or reveal something to you?

DID YOU KNOW

Did you know that former safety and NFL Hall of Famer John Lynch began his collegiate career at Stanford as a quarterback?

The Longest Long Shot

History was made at Churchill Downs in Louisville, Kentucky, back in 2022, as Rich Strike won the 148th running of the Kentucky Derby as the biggest long shot out of the twenty horses in the race (80 to 1 odds). The only horse to ever win this race with longer odds (91–1) was Donerail in 1911.

According to SI.com, Rich Strike became only the second horse to win the Kentucky Derby from the 20th post position since the present-day starting gate was initiated in 1930, joining Big Brown in 2008.

Also, before this victory, the horse had only won one other race in his career and didn't even finish second during his previous five starts. Not only was Rich Strike a long shot to win the race, but he was also a long shot to even be in the race.

Heading into Derby week he was only an alternate. It wasn't until thirty seconds before the deadline that he entered the twenty-horse field after Ethereal Road pulled out of the race.

As improbable as this win was, Rich Strike's trainer, Eric Reed, put it this way after the race: "Small trainer. Small rider. Small stable. We should have been 80-to-1. But I knew what I had. I knew what we had and what it was capable of, and if he ran good, anything could happen."[1]

---

1.   Dana O'Neil, "'What Planet Are We On?' A Horse Like Rich Strike Isn't

Many of us today are at the "starting gates," beginning our day facing a battle that appears impossible to win. Victory feels like such a long shot right now, and we're looking for answers, praying for God to move, and facing "80-to-1 odds."

Everything suggests how improbable our circumstances are to turn out in a good way, and getting a win in our current "20th post position" seems unlikely.

However, these are the predicaments where God shows up in glorious, remarkable, miraculous ways. We have to remember that we serve a God who has shown up over and over in the past. He can accomplish the impossible, do the unimaginable, and help us overcome the longest of long-shot situations.

In Jeremiah 32:27, God says, "Behold, I am the LORD, the God of all flesh. Is anything too hard for Me?" (ESV).

Luke 1:37 assures us that "nothing will be impossible with God" (ESV).

And in Matthew 19:26, Jesus told his disciples that "with God everything is possible.'"

When we're in the middle of our seemingly impossible challenges, we need to recite these verses and choose to believe in God's incredible power. We must trust that He's able to do anything and that He will when it's part of His plan.

Rich Strike's trainer, Eric Reed said, "I knew what we had and what it was capable of, and if he ran good, anything could happen."[2] Similarly, we know Who we have in God and what He's capable of, and with His goodness and power, anything can happen!

Together, let's declare, "'Ah, Lord GOD! It is you who have made the heavens and the earth by your great power and by your outstretched arm! Nothing is too hard for You'" (Jeremiah 32:17 ESV).

Supposed to Win the Kentucky Derby," *Athletic,* May 7, 2022, https://theathletic.com/3299361/2022/05/07/long-shot-rich-strike-wins-kentucky-derby/.

2. O'Neil, "'What Planet Are We On?'"

I'm Bryce Johnson, and you can *UNPACK* that!

PRAYER: *Heavenly Father, I believe in Your power and goodness. I trust You to do improbable things in my life and want to give You all the glory and honor. I know nothing is too hard for You, so I trust You to come through in amazing ways. My hope is in You and You alone. In Jesus' name I pray. Amen.*

When has God previously shown up when what you were hoping for seemed like a long shot?

What impossible situation today feels hopeless unless God intervenes?

DID YOU KNOW

Did you know that the first winner of the Kentucky Derby was Aristides, who won the title in 1875?

Tom Brady's Stolen Jersey

An unexpected and somewhat strange storyline emerged in the hours after New England's improbable comeback win over the Atlanta Falcons in Super Bowl 51.

Shortly after the Patriots completed one of the greatest comebacks in sports history, social media started buzzing with reports that someone had stolen New England quarterback Tom Brady's jersey.

The league immediately began investigating the incident and discovered the jersey was stolen by a media member who got his credential request approved thanks to a previous job he had held at a newspaper.

The man had simply slipped into the Patriots' locker room and casually pulled the jersey out of Brady's bag during the postgame celebration.

This surprising situation leads us to ask these questions:

How could someone enter the Patriots' locker room and walk out with the jersey in hand?

Where was security?

Why wasn't anyone guarding Brady's stuff?

Why was this kind of access given?

This occurrence resulted in necessary changes, as the NFL focused even more attention on protecting its players and doing a better job of tracking who is going in and out of the locker rooms.

I think this debacle can be a wake-up call for us too.

Are we aware of what we're letting into our minds and hearts each day?

Are we guarding our thoughts?

Are we allowing media, culture, TV, music, or movies to alter our views and affect our character?

Are we giving negative thoughts and emotions access to our hearts and minds?

What kind of effect are the people we've invited into our lives having on us?

We must recognize the danger of filling our minds and hearts with negativity and harmful thoughts and attitudes because once let in, greater damage can be done. Our actions flow from our hearts and what we think about, so we must stay alert and be on guard.

Proverbs 4:23 tells us, "Guard your heart above all else, for it determines the course of your life."

Sometimes we can fall into the trap of believing that "anything in moderation" is okay, but that's not always true if we're opening ourselves up to something that is potentially harmful. Also, it doesn't take very much for a negative influence to produce toxic results in the life of a believer. Galatians 5:9 says, "A little yeast works through the whole batch of dough" (NIV).

As followers of Jesus, we must heed the counsel found in Colossians 3:1–3: "Since you have been raised to new life with Christ, set your sights on the realities of heaven, where Christ sits in the place of honor at God's right hand. Think about the things of heaven, not the things of earth. For you died to this life, and your real life is hidden with Christ in God."

The battle of the mind is a daily fight, but thankfully we know, with God's strength, we can remain watchful and careful about what and whom we allow entry into our lives.

Let's choose to place importance on protecting our hearts and minds. If we are filled with God's truth, our joy and peace will not be stolen.

I'm Bryce Johnson, and you can *UNPACK* that!

PRAYER: *Heavenly Father, I pray I will place importance on protecting my heart and mind and being aware of what I'm allowing into my life. Please give me the strength to reject the negative things of this earth, so I can focus on the realities of heaven and my new life in Christ. It's in Jesus' name I pray. Amen.*

In what ways have you allowed an opening for negative things or people to enter your life?

What are some practical ways to better guard your mind and heart?

 **DID YOU KNOW**

Did you know that Tom Brady currently has twice as many playoff wins (35) as any other quarterback in NFL history?

Contemplating Death

The sports world was rocked by the tragic passing of NBA legend Kobe Bryant early in 2020. The news of Bryant's death was painful—and yet, this very sad accident had a positive impact on many people.

Unfortunately, it often takes a death for us to consider what matters most and to make necessary changes in our lives.

Specifically, the message that was shared following Kobe's death was one of forgiveness and reconciliation and of embracing both before it's too late.

The suddenness of Kobe dying reminded us how fragile life is and how quickly we can lose someone we care about. That reminder should give us a sense of urgency to forgive and reconcile without delaying another day.

ESPN analyst Jay Williams brought this up while sharing his thoughts about Kobe on Facebook. He encouraged his viewers to let go of whatever they have against someone.[1]

Former NBA center Kendrick Perkins, who had been feuding with Kevin Durant on Twitter, put an end to the beef by tweeting: "Just wanted to tell you I Love you my brother and whatever I did to hurt you I'm sorry bro and hope you forgive me!!! I love you, bro . . . !"

---

1. See the video "Jay Williams Reflects on the Life of Kobe Bryant" and Williams's January 6, 2020, comment on the ESPN Facebook page, https://www.facebook.com/ESPN/videos/jay-williams-reflects-on-the-life-of-kobe-bryant/183289106100048/.

Perkins went on to explain how his friendship with Durant was more valuable than keeping a Twitter beef going. He shared, "I also wanted the world to see that, hey, if you have a problem with a loved one, a friend, a family member, or whoever, hey, life is too short. The next sixty seconds is not promised. Nip that in the bud and heal those wounds with those people that you love and get past it. And that's what I wanted to do. And I wanted to reach out to KD to let him know, like, I love you, bro, and I'm not afraid to let the world see that I love you."[2]

Contemplating death causes us to think differently and change our perspective, so hopefully those thoughts can lead us to a desire to forgive and reconcile with others.

As followers of Jesus, we should be allowing forgiveness and grace to flow from us, because His death on the cross changed everything. When we contemplate Jesus' death (and resurrection) and the gift of salvation He made available to us, it changes our perspective on forgiveness.

God shows us undeserved grace by forgiving us and setting us free from the penalty of sin so we, in turn, can forgive those who hurt us.

Ephesians 4:31–32 tells us, " Let all bitterness and wrath and anger and clamor [perpetual animosity, resentment, strife, fault-finding] and slander be put away from you, along with every kind of malice [all spitefulness, verbal abuse, malevolence]. Be kind and helpful to one another, tender-hearted [compassionate, understanding], forgiving one another [readily and freely], just as God in Christ also forgave you" (AMP). Although that's hard to do, espe-

---

2. Jacob Camenker, "Boston Celtic's Kendrick Perkins Explains How Kobe Bryant's Passing Made Him Squash Beef with Kevin Durant," *Sports Boston*, updated January 28, 2020, https://www.nbcsportsboston.com/nba/boston-celtics-kendrick-perkins-explains-how-kobe-bryants-passing-made-him-squash-beef-with-kevin-durant/337881.

cially when the pain is so deep, let's be encouraged to stop waiting, since we know how fragile this life is.

Jesus made a way for us to be forgiven, and He also made a way for us to forgive.

Together, let's look to the cross as a reminder of the forgiveness we've been given and rely on Him to provide the strength and power we need to move forward and forgive others.

I'm Bryce Johnson, and you can *UNPACK* that!

PRAYER: *Heavenly Father, I'm filled with thankfulness for the grace and forgiveness You've shown me. Please allow me to forgive those who hurt me. Help me ask for forgiveness from those I've hurt. I desire to have reconciled relationships and need Your strength and healing power. In Jesus' name I pray. Amen.*

Who is someone you need to forgive? Whom do you need to ask for forgiveness?

Why is our understanding of God's grace critical in allowing us to forgive others?

DID YOU KNOW

Did you know that Kobe Bryant holds the NBA record for most points scored in a single arena, having scored 16,161 points at the Staples Center?

Tough Conversations

After going through a full training camp and preseason, over 1,000 players are informed they didn't make the final 53-man roster as the regular season begins.

The coaching staff and front office are tasked with determining who should or shouldn't make the limited roster. This whole process is part of the unfortunate but necessary business side of the NFL.

It must be very difficult for coaches to look players in the eye and tell them they didn't make the cut. Although it's what coaches have to do, genuine emotions, relationships, and lives are involved when these tough conversations take place.

As uncomfortable as these conversations are, teams need to move forward and allow players to know where they stand. If coaches communicate the reasons for their decisions, players can benefit from knowing what to work on moving forward and embrace being cut as an opportunity to go in a different direction.

Coaches likely have different approaches to handling these difficult conversations. However, they all need to be confident and willing to tell players what they don't want to hear but need to hear. Hopefully, even though it's football, the coaches do so with kindness, gratitude, empathy, and compassion.

Whether at work, at home, at church, or in our neighborhoods, we probably don't like having tough conversations. They're usually required, however, to clear the air, help someone, or allow both sides to move on.

As followers of Jesus, we're called to have three specific conversations with people in our lives . . . and often, they're uncomfortable to have.

First, we're called to confess our sins to one another. James 5:16 tells us to "admit [our] faults to one another and pray for each other so that [we] may be healed. The earnest prayer of a righteous man has great power and wonderful results" (TLB).

Second, we must be willing to confront and come alongside fellow believers who are caught up in sin. Galatians 6:1 says, "Brothers, if anyone is caught in any sin, you who are spiritual [that is, you who are responsive to the guidance of the Spirit] are to restore such a person in a spirit of gentleness [not with a sense of superiority or self-righteousness], keeping a watchful eye on yourself, so that you are not tempted as well" (AMP).

Finally, we're called to communicate the gospel of Jesus Christ. Jesus gives us this challenge in Mark 16:15: "You are to go into all the world and preach the Good News to everyone, everywhere." (TLB).

The interactions that take place in these situations can involve genuine emotions, while relationships and lives are affected by having these challenging conversations. The key for us is to have the proper approach and always ask God to give us wisdom and the right words to say. We want to be honest while having compassion, grace, and humility.

Colossians 4:6 urges us, "Let your conversation be gracious and attractive so that you will have the right response for everyone."

Instead of avoiding these difficult conversations out of fear, we need to ask God for boldness and confidence to embrace them, so everyone can experience the benefits that result from speaking the truth in love.

Let's be mindful that tough conversations allow us to know where each other stands. Let's allow this kind of communication to lead to healing, growth, and an opportunity to move forward in a new direction.

I'm Bryce Johnson, and you can *UNPACK* that!

PRAYER: *Heavenly Father, please help me to embrace the important, yet tough conversations in life. I pray You'll give me the right words to say at the right time and approach these conversations with honesty, humility, and grace. I ask that there will be healing and growth. In Jesus' name I pray. Amen.*

What conversations are the toughest for you to have?

What growth or healing have you experienced following a difficult conversation?

 **DID YOU KNOW**

Did you know that Hall of Fame quarterback Johnny Unitas was cut by the Pittsburgh Steelers after being selected in the ninth round of the 1956 Draft?

Day Twenty-Nine

You Can't Win on Thursday, But You Can Lose

If you're a professional golfer who wants to win a major tournament, you have to get off to a good start on Thursday, the day the tournament begins.

The proverbial saying "You can't win the tournament on Thursday, but you can lose it" has proven to be true time and again over the years. No player has ever solidified victory after just one round of play, but countless players have ensured that they would not be in contention after a poor showing to start their tournament.

"You can't win the tournament on Thursday, but you can lose it" is a saying that also rings true concerning life on earth, eternity, and experiencing victory.

The reality is, we can't win by having "an impressive round" on earth, because, in the larger scheme of things, it's only "Thursday."

When we think we're winning based on temporary worldly standards, such as money, fame, power, or acclaim, it's a short-sighted perspective because this life is just "Thursday." What we do on "Thursday" does matter, but our greater concern must be what happens next.

Matthew 16:26 asks these important questions: "For what will it profit a man if he gains the whole world [wealth, fame, success],

113

but forfeits his soul? Or what will a man give in exchange for his soul?" (AMP).

In the end, it's all about experiencing victory through Jesus and understanding that eternity is what truly matters. A golfer knows that leading the field on Thursday pales in comparison to victory on Sunday.

We also must remember we can't win by our performance on "Thursday"—that is, by trying to earn our way to heaven (Sunday) based on what we do here on earth. What we do in our own strength and power on "Thursday" will never be enough because eternal life is only available through faith in Jesus Christ.

Ephesians 2:8–9 tells us, "It is by grace you have been saved, through faith—and this is not from yourselves, it is the gift of God—not by works, so that no one can boast" (NIV).

Although we can't win with the "best score" on "Thursday," what happens while we're here on earth can cause us to lose if we say no to Jesus and decide not to believe in Him. We can lose both our souls and eternal life by not surrendering to Jesus and placing our faith in Him for the forgiveness of our sins. If we choose not to repent and instead live life according to our own way in pursuit of "Thursday" success apart from Jesus, then we lose and miss the cut.

Thankfully, once we surrender to Jesus and receive His grace on "Thursday," we know we've won on "Sunday" because our eternal victory is secure. From then on, throughout the rest of the "tournament," the life we live is like that of the apostle Paul. He explained in Galatians 2:20, "My old self has been crucified with Christ. It is no longer I who live, but Christ lives in me. So I live in this earthly body by trusting in the Son of God, who loved me and gave himself for me."

As followers of Jesus, we live in victory both now and for eternity . . . from "Thursday to Sunday."

I'm Bryce Johnson, and you can *UNPACK* that!

PRAYER: *Heavenly Father, I'm so grateful that my salvation is not based on my performance and that this life isn't all there is. I long to spend eternity with You, and while I'm still here on earth, I pray that I won't chase temporary satisfaction or be distracted by worldly pursuits, but instead live in view of eternity. In Jesus' name I pray. Amen.*

In what ways do you get caught up in "winning Thursday" based on the world's standards?

In what ways would your life change if you lived based on the fact that you've already won on "Sunday" because of Jesus?

DID YOU KNOW

Did you know that Paul Lawrie has the record for the biggest comeback in the final round of a major tournament, winning The Open in 1999 after entering 10 shots back?

Day Thirty

Proceed with Caution

Michael Vick remains one of the most electrifying and dynamic quarterbacks the NFL has ever seen on the field, despite his choices off it. Watching him run and make defenders miss was exciting, as he put his body on the line every time he left the pocket.

Just as Vick risked injury when hitting the open field, current running NFL quarterback Lamar Jackson faces a similar dilemma as a skilled rusher who has an aggressive running style.

Jackson has already gone over 1,000 yards rushing in a season multiple times in his professional career, and he has firmly established himself as a threat to run and have great success with his legs anytime he drops back to pass.

However, as successful as Jackson has been at rushing the ball, there is concern that a quarterback running the ball too much is not sustainable and might open the door for an increased number of injuries.

Vick, who undoubtedly understands the toll it takes on a quarterback, shared the following wisdom and warning for Jackson in an interview with ESPN.com: "With quarterbacks, we're not used to getting hit all the time. When we do it, it can either get you into the game or it can shake you up a little bit. It's not like a guy sitting in the pocket, you run the risk of getting injured. I'm not saying that should deter Lamar or scare him; I'm just saying proceed with caution."[1]

This is sage advice coming from a player who understands the desire to run and make plays while also realizing the dangers. Vick is leveraging his experience, and hopefully, Jackson and other quarterbacks hear the message to "proceed with caution."

Likewise, we've all been given plenty of warnings throughout our lives. Some we seem to take to heart, and others we blow off. Unfortunately, it's easy to respond with,

"That won't happen to me."

"Yeah, that may have been true for you, but I'm different."

"I hear what you're saying, but this is my only option."

"I've got it under control, it won't be a problem."

The truth is, warnings and advice are given to protect us. They are shared with us by an expert or someone who has been through something already. It's up to us to be wise and humble enough to listen and "proceed with caution."

The Bible is filled with warnings and wisdom that are intended to help us live a fulfilling life found in Jesus. God created us and is all-knowing, so it's in our best interest to be obedient and follow His Word.

Proverbs, the book of wisdom, shares these two important verses:

Pride ends in destruction; humility ends in honor. (18:12 TLB)

There is a way that seems right to a man, but its end is the way to death. (14:12 ESV)

---

1. Jamison Hensley, "Michael Vick's Advice to Raven's QB Lamar Jackson: 'Proceed with Caution,'" ESPN, November 27, 2018, https://www.espn.com/nfl/story/_/id/25395321/michael-vick-advice-baltimore-ravens-qb-lamar-jackson-proceed-caution.

When we humble ourselves and openly accept advice and warnings, we're able to avoid many pitfalls. This way we have a better understanding of how often to "run up the field" and when to "remain in the pocket."

We can learn from those who have gone before us and listen to the Lord's leading each day. Let's look outside of ourselves for wisdom and knowledge, instead of thinking we've got it all figured out on our own.

I'm Bryce Johnson, and you can *UNPACK* that!

PRAYER: *Heavenly Father, forgive me for my pride and unwillingness to listen to wise advice. I pray that I will heed the warnings You have for me and live according to Your will. In Jesus' name I pray. Amen.*

What is the best advice or the greatest warning you've received?

When was a time you went against someone's advice or warning but wish you had listened?

DID YOU KNOW

Did you know that Michael Vick holds the NFL record for most rushing yards by a quarterback, totaling 6,109 yards during his career?

NEXT STEPS

Connect with the UNPACKIN' it Community of sports fans following Jesus!

Enjoy more devotionals and other content from UNPACKIN' it Ministries.

www.unpackinit.com

I hope this book challenged, encouraged, and inspired you to follow Jesus and become more like Him. It's my prayer that you would pass the book along to others and get copies for your friends and family.

As you continue in your faith journey, I hope you will connect with UNPACKIN' it Ministries, a ministry for sports fans that began in 2014. In addition to this book of devotionals, we also send new faith and sports devotionals out Monday, Wednesday, and Friday through email. We unpack spiritual truths and relatable parallels from the sports world to help readers grow in their faith. Each day's devotional focuses on relevant scripture and closes with a short prayer.

*Subscribe TODAY at unpackinit.com/subscribe.

UNPACKIN' it Ministries offers numerous five-day reading plans on the popular Bible reading app. While unpacking sports through a lens of faith and Biblical truth, you'll be challenged, encouraged, and inspired as a sports fan to follow Jesus and become more like Him.

*Download the YouVersion app on your mobile device and search for "UNPACKIN' it."

We also offer opportunities for sports fans to experience fellowship through gatherings, small groups, and events. I invite you to get involved with our other ministry initiatives which include Fantasy Football Fellowship and Sports Fan Fellowship.

Another way our ministry uses sports parallels that relate to life and faith is through conversations on *The UNPACKIN' it Podcast* which can be watched on YouTube and social media or listened to on any podcast platform. We unpack big sports stories, impactful faith journeys, and the ups and downs of life with intriguing athletes, coaches, media personalities, and ministry leaders.

*Subscribe using your favorite podcast platform or visit unpackinit.com/podcast.

My passion is to see sports fans everywhere following Jesus and doing so in community with other sports fans. Thanks for reading this book…to God be all the glory, honor and praise!

Facebook.com/unpackinit

youtube.com/unpackinit

Let us know how God moved in your life while reading this book by emailing Bryce@thesportsdevotional.com.

A Sports Fan's Prayer

I *pray that I put more faith in Jesus*
than in my favorite player.

I *pray that I have more passion for sharing the gospel*
than celebrating a championship win.

I *pray that I find more joy in Christ*
than in seeing my team score in the final seconds of a game.

I *pray that I am more committed to following Jesus*
than stats and scores.

I *pray that I place more trust in God's Word*
than in sports media.

I *pray that I'm more dedicated to my family and friends*
than watching my favorite team play.

I *pray that I have peace that surpasses all understanding*
even during a losing season.

I *pray that I get angrier about injustice in the world*
than I do about a ref's bad call.

I *pray that I believe God is a God of miracles*
even beyond the court and field.

I *pray that I embrace real winning*
as receiving God's grace and forgiveness.

In *Jesus' name, I watch and pray ... A M E N!*

SCAN HERE to learn more about Invite Press, a premier publishing imprint created to invite people to a deeper faith and living relationship with Jesus Christ.